BASEBALL IN THE
AMERICAN LEAGUE EAST
DIVISION

BALTIMORE

ORIOLES

BOSTON

RED SOX

NEW YORK

YANKEES

TAMPA BAY

RAYS

TORONTO

BLUE JAYS

rosen publishing's
rosen
central®

New York

MATT MONTEVERDE

For Mom and Dad

Published in 2009 by The Rosen Publishing Group, Inc.
29 East 21st Street, New York, NY 10010

First Edition

Library of Congress Cataloging-in-Publication Data

Monteverde, Matthew.
Baseball in the American League East Division / Matt Monteverde.
    p. cm.—(Inside major league baseball)
Includes bibliographical references and index.
ISBN-13: 978-1-4358-5040-8 (library binding)
ISBN-13: 978-1-4358-5414-7 (pbk)
ISBN-13: 978-1-4358-5420-8 (6 pack)
1. American League of Professional Baseball Clubs—History—Juvenile literature.
2. Baseball teams—United States—Juvenile literature. I. Title.
GV875.A15M66 2009
796.3570973—dc22

        2008019929

Manufactured in the United States of America

On the cover: Baseball cards, top to bottom: Nick Markakis of the Baltimore Orioles; Jonathan Papelbon of the Boston Red Sox; Alex Rodriguez of the New York Yankees; Carl Crawford of the Tampa Bay Rays; Roy Halladay of the Toronto Blue Jays. Foreground: New York Yankees' Derek Jeter. Background: Boston's Fenway Park.

CONTENTS

INTRODUCTION

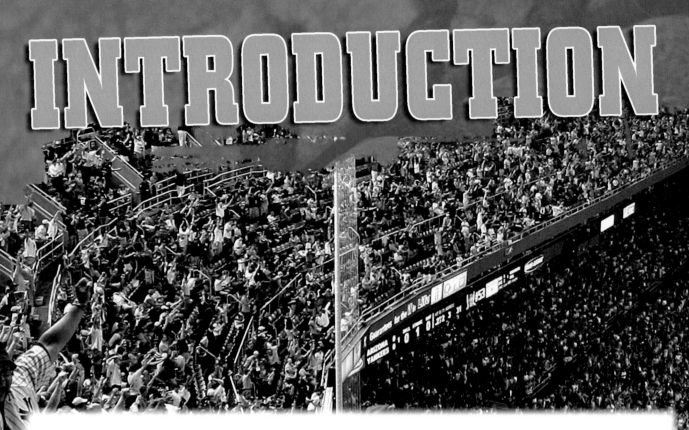

The game of baseball is considered the "great American pastime," embraced by generations of fans for well over a century. Considering how baseball has changed over the years, it is interesting that children, parents, and grandparents can all enjoy the game. And baseball continues to evolve to this day. One of the biggest differences in Major League Baseball today compared to the past is how the teams are now organized.

Currently, there are 30 teams in the major leagues. They are organized into two leagues, the American League and the National League. In comparison, there were only 20 teams in 1968. In 1969, the league grew by four teams, bringing the total number of teams to 24. In order to adapt to the addition of these teams, the two leagues were split into divisions. These were the American League East, American League West, National League East, and National League West. These divisions are still in existence today. In 1994, two more divisions were added, the American League Central and the National

League Central. Teams were moved from the existing divisions to create the new Central divisions. Teams are placed into the divisions based on the geographical location of their home city.

Of the six divisions in Major League Baseball, the American League East—commonly called the AL East—is arguably the one with the richest history. The AL East is home to two of the most storied teams in all of baseball, the Boston Red Sox and the New York Yankees. In addition to the Red Sox

Background: View of Yankee Stadium from the upper deck of the right-field bleacher seats.
Above: Red Sox slugger David Ortiz is one of the top hitters in the AL East.

and Yankees, the AL East includes the Baltimore Orioles. Their home stadium, Camden Yards, is relatively new but is widely admired for its classic ballpark look and feel. The division also has a modern flavor with the Toronto Blue Jays and Tampa Bay Rays, who both play in domed stadiums. Read on to learn more about the teams, players, ballparks, and baseball history of the American League East.

CHAPTER ONE
THE EARLY YEARS: 1969–1979

The American League East division was founded in 1969. The original teams of the AL East were the Baltimore Orioles, Boston Red Sox, Cleveland Indians, Detroit Tigers, New York Yankees, and Washington Senators. When play began in the AL East, it quickly became apparent that the Orioles had the talent to dominate the early years of the division. From 1969 to 1971, manager Earl Weaver led the Orioles

Above, left: Baltimore Orioles third baseman Brooks Robinson, in 1970. Background: Fenway Park's famous Green Monster wall in left field.

to three AL East titles and World Series appearances. During this span, the Orioles fielded strong teams that included future Hall of Famers Brooks Robinson, Frank Robinson, and Jim Palmer. Although the Orioles reached the World Series in three consecutive seasons, they won it only once, in 1970, playing against the Cincinnati Reds.

Realignment of the AL East

Big changes occurred in the AL East during the 1972 season. First, the Washington Senators moved to Texas, and the team became known as the Rangers. As the team was no longer located on the East Coast, the Rangers joined the AL West division. At the same time, the Milwaukee Brewers moved from the AL West to the AL East. Along with a new lineup of teams in the AL East came new results. For the first time in the short history of the division, the Orioles did not win the AL East. Instead, they finished in third place, behind both Detroit and Boston. Detroit rose to the top of the division behind their pitching ace, Mickey Lolich, who went 22–14 with a 2.50 ERA.

Yankees–Red Sox Rivalry

In the mid-1970s, New York and Boston battled for the top spot in the AL East. The rivalry between the Yankees and the Red Sox, one of the best in all of sports, dates back to the early 1900s. It's natural that a rivalry would develop, as New York and Boston are only a short distance away from each other and both teams have always competed within the same division.

In 1975, the Red Sox won the division and advanced to the World Series, only to lose to the Cincinnati Reds in seven games. In 1976,

American League East Team History
(since realignment in 1994)

	YEAR ENTERED THE AL EAST	AL EAST CHAMPIONSHIPS	AMERICAN LEAGUE PENNANTS	WORLD SERIES CHAMPIONSHIPS
New York Yankees	1969	11*	6	4
Boston Red Sox	1969	2	2	2
Baltimore Orioles	1969	1	0	0
Toronto Blue Jays	1977	0	0	0
Tampa Bay Rays	1998	0	0	0

* Includes 1994; New York was leading the division when the season was cut short by the players' strike.

however, the Yankees took the AL East title. They advanced to the World Series but were swept by the Reds.

In 1977, the Yankees once again topped the Red Sox and returned to the World Series. With the help of newly acquired free agent out-fielder Reggie Jackson, the Yankees defeated the Los Angeles Dodgers, four games to two, in the 1977 World Series. Jackson was the star of the series, hitting three home runs in game 6 (on three consecutive pitches!). To this day, Jackson remains the only player in baseball

Reggie Jackson *(right)* watches his third home run leave the park in game 6 of the 1977 World Series. The Yankees beat the Dodgers 8–4 to win the franchise's 21st world title.

history to hit three home runs in a single World Series game. Jackson's powerful postseason hitting earned him the nickname "Mr. October."

Blue Jays Join the AL East

The Toronto Blue Jays joined the AL East in 1977 as an expansion team. At the time, the Blue Jays joined the Montreal Expos of the National League as the only two teams to play their home games in Canada. The Expos have since moved to Washington, D.C., and are now called the Nationals. As a result, the Blue Jays are currently the only Canadian team in Major League Baseball.

Like most expansion teams, the Blue Jays did not fare too well in their first few years of existence. During their first year of play, they finished in last place in the AL East. They remained in last place for the remainder of the 1970s. Fortunately for the Blue Jays and their fans, the team improved greatly in the mid-1980s and became a top contender in the division.

Colorful Pitchers of the AL East

Jim Palmer of the Orioles, one of the best pitchers ever, had some great years in the 1970s. In the eight seasons between 1970 and 1977, he won 20 games seven times. Although he was a brilliant Hall of Fame pitcher, Palmer did not call much attention to himself. However, several of baseball's most interesting characters pitched for AL East teams in the 1970s. Not surprisingly, a few of these players had colorful nicknames to go along with their interesting personalities.

Mark "The Bird" Fidrych

In 1976, Mark "The Bird" Fidrych burst onto the Major League Baseball scene with the Detroit Tigers. He dazzled fans with his incredible pitching skills and baffled them with his unusual antics on the mound. Fidrych got his nickname because his tall, lanky frame was similar to that of Big Bird, the *Sesame Street* character. Fidrych won the American League Rookie of the Year Award in 1976, but he was perhaps more famous for his unusual behavior on the pitcher's mound. During games, he would often strut around the mound or pat the dirt while talking to

Bucky Dent and the "Boston Massacre"

The longtime Yankees–Red Sox rivalry had one of its more memorable episodes during the 1978 season. In late July, the Red Sox had a comfortable nine-game lead over second-place Milwaukee and a fourteen-game lead over the Yankees. Then, in one of the greatest comebacks in baseball history, the red-hot Yankees battled back into contention. As the season wound down in September, the Yankees headed to Fenway Park to take on the Sox in a four-game series. Not only did the Yanks sweep the Sox in the series, but they beat them by a combined score of 42–9! The series defeat was so crushing to the Red Sox and their fans that it became known as the "Boston Massacre." Just as important, it helped the Yankees tie the Red Sox atop the AL East at the conclusion of the regular season.

With the two teams tied for first place, a one-game play-off was scheduled to break the tie. The winner of the game would head to the American League Championship Series (ALCS), while the losing team would see its season come to a bitter end. Late in the game, played at Fenway Park, the Red Sox were up on the Yankees 2–0. Then, in the seventh inning, with the Yankees' hopes fading, light-hitting shortstop Bucky Dent came to bat. Incredibly, he hit a two-out, three-run home run that barely made it over the famous Green Monster wall in left field, giving the Yankees a 3–2 lead. The Yankees, with the help of Dent's historic home run, held on to win the game 5–4. New York went on to play Los Angeles in the World Series for the second straight year. Just as they did in the 1977 World Series, the Yankees defeated the Dodgers in six games, taking home their second straight championship.

himself. Even stranger, he would sometimes talk to the baseball before pitching it!

Luis Tiant, "El Tiante"

Cuban-born Luis Tiant was a star pitcher for the Red Sox from 1971 to 1978, and for the Yankees from 1979 to 1980. The pitcher's animated

Detroit Tigers pitcher Mark "The Bird" Fidrych was one of baseball's most colorful characters in the 1970s. His bizarre behavior included patting and smoothing out the mound between pitches.

pitching style and likeable personality made him an instant fan favorite. On the field, Tiant was one of the most competitive players in the game. Off the field, the chubby Tiant displayed an easygoing demeanor highlighted by his glowing smile. Besides his unique pitching style, Tiant was well known for his love of smoking cigars. In fact, in 2005 he started a cigar wholesaler called El Tiante Cigars, based in Massachusetts. Their bestselling line of cigars is called "23," the number Tiant wore with the Red Sox.

Luis Tiant's unusual delivery kept opposing hitters off balance. Here, Tiant is pitching in 1974, a season in which he won 22 games and threw seven shutouts.

Rich "Goose" Gossage

Rich "Goose" Gossage was a dominant relief pitcher for the New York Yankees in the late 1970s and early 1980s. With his burly frame and big Fu Manchu mustache, Gossage was one of the most intimidating pitchers of his era. He threw a blazing fastball that approached 100 miles per hour (161 kilometers per hour). Gossage made nine All-Star teams in his career and pitched in three World Series, two of them with the Yankees. He led the American League in saves three times, in 1975, 1978, and 1980. His 27 saves and 2.01 ERA in 1978 earned him the Relief Man of the Year Award. Unlike today's closers, who usually pitch only one inning, Gossage often threw two or three innings to earn a save.

Gossage often glared at hitters from the pitcher's mound and was not afraid to throw at them if they were crowding home plate. Gossage was called "Goose" because he stuck his neck out like a goose while peering in at the catcher's sign. Gossage was elected to the Hall of Fame in 2007.

CHAPTER TWO

A LEVEL PLAYING FIELD:
1980–1989

In the 1980s, there was no team that dominated the AL East like the Orioles and Yankees had in the 1970s. This was largely due to free agency. Until the mid-1970s, teams had the exclusive option to re-sign their players to new contracts when the old one expired. But then a rule change allowed players with expired contracts (free agents) to join any team they liked, usually the highest bidder.

Above, left: Cal Ripken became known as baseball's "Iron Man." He earned the nickname by playing for more than 15 seasons without missing a game.

Players who played their entire careers on one team, such as Joe DiMaggio, Ted Williams, Mickey Mantle, and Brooks Robinson, became a rarity after 1980.

Even Competition in the AL East

In 1982, the Milwaukee Brewers were the surprise winners of the AL East. Not usually a serious contender for the division title up until that point, the Brewers enjoyed the most successful season in franchise history. Future Hall of Famers Robin Yount, Paul Molitor, and Rollie Fingers

In 1982, Robin Yount helped the Milwaukee Brewers reach the World Series. The Brewers later moved from the AL East to the AL Central, and they now play in the National League Central division.

led the Brewers to the team's first World Series appearance. The young Brewers team failed to win their first World Series title, however, as they lost to the St. Louis Cardinals in seven games.

The two most successful teams of the AL East during the 1980s were the 1983 Orioles and the 1984 Tigers. The 1983 Orioles team included future Hall of Famers Cal Ripken, Eddie Murray, and Jim Palmer. They defeated the Philadelphia Phillies four games to one in the World Series. The 1984 Tigers were a gritty team, led by future

Hall of Fame manager Sparky Anderson. Star players Kirk Gibson, Lou Whitaker, Alan Trammell, and pitcher Jack Morris helped the Tigers defeat the San Diego Padres in the World Series four games to one.

Rogers Centre: Baseball's Stadium of the Future

The Blue Jays' home stadium, called Rogers Centre, was probably baseball's most futuristic, cutting-edge stadium when it was built in

This photo of Rogers Centre in Toronto, Canada, offers a good view of the stadium's retractable roof. The hi-tech videoboard in center field is one of the largest in North America, measuring 110 feet (34 meters) wide by 33 feet (10 meters) high.

the 1980s. The stadium was called SkyDome when it opened in 1989, and it was renamed Rogers Centre in 2005. Rogers Centre is perhaps most famous for having a retractable roof. This means that the giant roof of the stadium can be opened or closed, depending on the weather, to keep the artificial playing surface in good condition. Rogers Centre also has restaurants overlooking the field and even has a hotel inside the ballpark.

Star Rookies of the AL East

During the 1980s the AL East was a division rich with young talent. Cal Ripken, Wade Boggs, Don Mattingly, and Roger Clemens were among the biggest stars in baseball to begin their careers on an AL East team. Ripken, Boggs, and Mattingly each spent their entire career playing in the AL East. In addition, Roger Clemens pitched for three AL East teams during his career.

A Long One

Before they were stars together in the AL East, Cal Ripken and Wade Boggs played against each other in the longest game in professional baseball history. Ripken played for the Rochester Red Wings, the Baltimore Orioles' minor league team. Boggs played for the Pawtucket Red Sox, Boston's minor league team. The game began on April 18, 1981. The contest went into extra innings and was tied 2–2 after 32 innings. At that point, the umpires decided to suspend the game and finish it at a later date. The game was resumed on June 23, 1981. On that night, the Pawtucket Red Sox won the game, 3–2, with a run in the 33rd inning.

Cal Ripken

Cal Ripken made his major league debut in 1981, playing for the Baltimore Orioles. Ripken, just 20 years old at the time, played in 23 games during the 1981 season. The young star played both shortstop and third base. The following year, Ripken won the American League Rookie of the Year Award. He played his entire career with the Orioles, from 1981 to 2001, and was inducted into the Baseball Hall of Fame in 2007.

Wade Boggs

Wade Boggs was 24 years old when he made his major league debut for the Red Sox in 1982. Boggs played first base and third base during his rookie year. That year, he hit for an impressive .349 batting average. Boggs played his entire career in the AL East with the Red Sox, Yankees, and Devil Rays. He collected more than 3,000 hits in

The Bill Buckner Play

The setting for the bizarre Bill Buckner Play was game 6 of the 1986 World Series at Shea Stadium in New York. The Red Sox were ahead of the New York Mets in the series, three games to two. It was the bottom of the 10th inning, with two outs, and the Red Sox were ahead 5–3. Boston appeared to be on the verge of victory. They needed only one more out to win the game and capture their first World Series title since 1918. However, the Red Sox bullpen failed to get the final out, and the Mets tied the game 5–5. Then, with a runner on second base, Mets outfielder Mookie Wilson hit a weak ground ball toward Red Sox first baseman Bill Buckner. Buckner tried to field the ball, but it rolled past his glove, through his legs, and into right field. The error allowed the Mets' Ray Knight to score the game-winning run. The next night at Shea Stadium, the Red Sox lost game 7 of the World Series 8–5.

his career and was inducted into the Baseball Hall of Fame in 2005.

Don Mattingly

Don Mattingly made his major league debut for the Yankees in 1982. Mattingly, nicknamed "Donnie Baseball," was 21 years old at the time. During the mid- to late 1980s, Mattingly was one of the best players in baseball. He won the AL batting title in 1984 and the AL MVP Award in 1985. Mattingly won nine Gold Glove Awards in his career as a first baseman. He retired from baseball after the 1995 season.

Don Mattingly was one of the best hitters in baseball during the 1980s. The Yankees retired his uniform number, 23, in 1997.

Roger Clemens

Roger Clemens, another star rookie for the Red Sox, made his major league debut in 1984, at twenty-one years old. Clemens played for four teams during his career, the Red Sox, Blue Jays, Yankees, and Astros. He won more than 350 games along with seven Cy Young Awards and is widely considered to be one of the best pitchers of all time.

American League East Award Winners
(since realignment in 1994)

American League MVP Award

1995: Mo Vaughn (Red Sox)
2005: Alex Rodriguez (Yankees)
2007: Alex Rodriguez (Yankees)

American League Rookie of the Year Award

1996: Derek Jeter (Yankees)
1997: Nomar Garciaparra (Red Sox)
2002: Eric Hinske (Blue Jays)
2007: Dustin Pedroia (Red Sox)

American League Cy Young Award

1996: Pat Hentgen (Blue Jays)
1997: Roger Clemens (Blue Jays)
1998: Roger Clemens (Blue Jays)
1999: Pedro Martinez (Red Sox)
2000: Pedro Martinez (Red Sox)
2001: Roger Clemens (Yankees)
2003: Roy Halladay (Blue Jays)

Rolaids Relief Man of the Year Award

1994: Lee Smith (Orioles)
1996: John Wetteland (Yankees)
1997: Randy Myers (Orioles)
1998: Tom Gordon (Red Sox)
1999: Mariano Rivera (Yankees)
2001: Mariano Rivera (Yankees)
2004: Mariano Rivera (Yankees)
2005: Mariano Rivera (Yankees)

World Series MVP Award

1996: John Wetteland (Yankees)
1998: Scott Brosius (Yankees)
1999: Mariano Rivera (Yankees)
2000: Derek Jeter (Yankees)
2004: Manny Ramirez (Red Sox)
2007: Mike Lowell (Red Sox)

The Toronto Blue Jays were the most successful team of the AL East in the early 1990s. The team made it to the World Series in 1992 and 1993. Games 3, 4, and 5 of the 1992 World Series were the first ever World Series games played outside of the United States. These games were played at SkyDome, the Blue Jays' state-of-the-art stadium in Toronto, Canada. Future Hall of Famer Dave Winfield, along with star players Roberto Alomar, Joe Carter,

Above, left: Joe Carter celebrates his walk-off home run in game 6 of the 1993 World Series. The blast gave the Blue Jays their second straight World Series title.

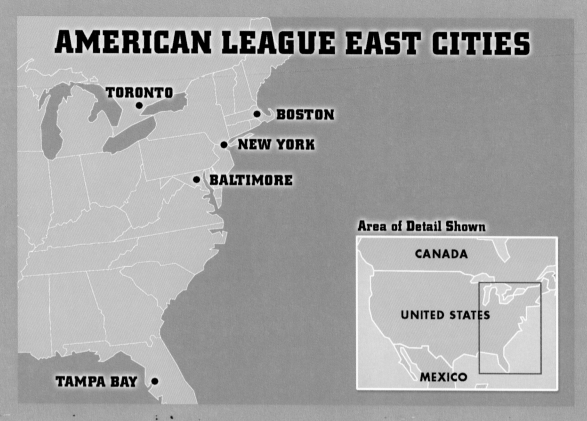

AMERICAN LEAGUE EAST CITIES

TORONTO

BOSTON

NEW YORK

BALTIMORE

TAMPA BAY

Area of Detail Shown

CANADA

UNITED STATES

MEXICO

The home cities of four of the five teams in the AL East are located in states bordering on the Atlantic Ocean. The fifth team, the Toronto Blue Jays, plays home games near Lake Ontario in Canada.

Jack Morris, and Juan Guzman, beat the Atlanta Braves in six games to win the team's first World Series championship.

In 1993, the Blue Jays came back even stronger than the 1992 championship team. They again won the AL East and advanced to the World Series. The Blue Jays led the 1993 World Series three games to two, but their hopes of a game 6 victory were bleak, as they trailed the Philadelphia Phillies 6–5 in the bottom of the ninth inning. With two out and men on base, Joe Carter came to bat against Phillies closer Mitch Williams. On a 2-2 count, Carter blasted a Williams pitch over the left-field wall for a walk-off home run. The Blue Jays, on one mighty swing of the bat from Joe Carter, took home the World Series trophy for the second straight year.

The Retro Stadium Craze

In 1992, a new stadium called Oriole Park at Camden Yards was built for the Baltimore Orioles. Instead of putting an emphasis on a futuristic look, like that of Rogers Centre, Camden Yards was built to remind fans and players of old-time ballparks such as Ebbets Field and the Polo Grounds. These small, cozy stadiums have a nostalgic feel to them. Since Oriole Park was built, teams around the major leagues have built stadiums of their own that try to capture the same old-time look. Additionally, the Yankees are building one of their own, which is scheduled to open in 2009. The Rays also hope to build a new stadium, possibly by 2012.

The Strike

The landscape of the AL East changed following the conclusion of the 1993 season. In 1994, the Indians and Brewers moved out of the AL East to the newly created AL Central. Unfortunately, that same year, Major League Baseball players began a work strike on August 12. The strike canceled the remainder of the 1994 regular season, the play-offs, the World Series, and even the beginning of the 1995 season.

The strike not only canceled many baseball games, but it also angered the fans. Many did not return to watching and attending games once play resumed in April 1995. Fortunately, a historic event occurred on September 8 in the 1995 season to help bring some of the

Despite pleas from baseball fans all over America, the 1994 season ground to a halt when players went on strike.

fans back. That night, at Camden Yards in Baltimore, Cal Ripken broke Lou Gehrig's streak of 2,131 consecutive games played. Many people felt that baseball needed a bright moment like this in order to get disgruntled fans interested in the game again.

The American League Division Series

Shortly after Cal Ripken's historic game, the Red Sox won the AL East during the shortened 144-game season, going on to play in the first-ever AL Division Series (ALDS). The ALDS are two best-of-five series played before the AL Championship Series (ALCS). Four teams qualify to play in the ALDS. The four teams include the division-winning teams of the AL East, AL Central, and AL West, plus an AL wild card team. The wild card team is the second-place team, from any division, with the best record. The two winners of the ALDS advance to play each other in the ALCS.

From the time the AL East was founded in 1969 until the 1993 play-offs, there was no wild card team. Instead, the winners of the AL

Yankees pitcher David Cone reacts after walking in a run in game 5 of the 1995 American League Division Series against the Seattle Mariners.

East and AL West played each other in the ALCS. Unfortunately for the Red Sox and wild card–winning Yankees, they became the first American League teams to lose in the ALDS. The Yankees lost their ALDS to the Seattle Mariners, and the Red Sox lost to the Cleveland Indians.

Yankees Begin Another Dynasty

The Yankees began their most recent dynasty run in 1996. During that year, standout players Bernie Williams, Paul O'Neill, Wade Boggs, and Derek Jeter helped the Yankees win the AL East. The Yankees then cruised past Baltimore and Texas to advance to the 1996 World Series. In the World Series, they defeated the Atlanta Braves, four games to two, to win their 23rd championship title.

In 1998, the AL East welcomed a new team for the first time since 1977—the Tampa Bay Devil Rays. Like most first-year teams, the Devil Rays finished the season in last place. In contrast, the Yankees fielded one of the greatest baseball teams of all time. Led by Derek Jeter, Mariano Rivera, Bernie Williams, David Wells, and Orlando Hernandez, the 1998 Yankees finished atop the AL East, winning 114 regular season games. Their dominance continued in the postseason, as they won the ALDS and ALCS. In the World Series, the Yankees swept the San Diego Padres, four games to none. Including their postseason victories, the Yankees won 125 games in 1998, the most ever in baseball history.

The Yankees followed their historic 1998 season with another AL East title and trip to the World Series in 1999. In the series, the Yankees easily defeated the Braves four games to none. The victory solidified the Yankees' status as the most successful American League team of the 1990s. During the decade, they won three World Series titles, more than any other team.

Amazing Feats in the AL East

The AL East has a long history of great players and exciting, intense rivalries. So, it's no surprise that many memorable and historic moments occurred in the AL East during the 1990s. Below are a few of the more noteworthy accomplishments.

Dave Stieb Pitches the First No-Hitter in Blue Jays History

Dave Stieb enjoyed a long, successful career as a Blue Jays starting pitcher. He pitched for the Blue Jays from 1979 to 1992. Stieb then returned to the Blue Jays in 1998 to close out his career. Stieb pitched his best game for the Blue Jays on September 2, 1990. On that day, he threw the first no-hitter in Blue Jays history, beating the Indians 3–0 at Cleveland Stadium.

Jim Abbott Pitches a No-Hitter for the Yankees

On September 4, 1993, Yankees pitcher Jim Abbott pitched a no-hitter against the Cleveland Indians. As impressive as it is to throw a no-hitter, Abbott's was even more amazing than usual: the pitcher was born with just one hand. Despite being born without a right hand, Abbott overcame his handicap and was a successful pitcher for several years in the major leagues.

Roger Clemens Fans Twenty

On September 18, 1996, Red Sox ace Roger Clemens achieved the rare feat of striking out 20 batters in a nine-inning game. Clemens, nick-named "the Rocket," pitched this historic game against the Tigers at Tiger Stadium. Amazingly, the game marked the second time in his career that Clemens struck out 20 batters in a game. He had also

Roger Clemens delivers a pitch in his historic 20-strikeout game against the Detroit Tigers on September 18, 1996.

struck out 20 batters in one game in 1986.

Wade Boggs Gets 3,000

On August 7, 1999, Devil Rays third baseman Wade Boggs joined the exclusive 3,000-hit club. Boggs's 3,000th hit came against the Cleveland Indians at Tropicana Field in St. Petersburg, Florida. The game marked the first and only time that a player hit a home run for his 3,000th hit. In recognition for Boggs' achievements as a member of the Devil Rays, the team retired his jersey number 12. Boggs is the only player in Devil Rays history to have his number retired.

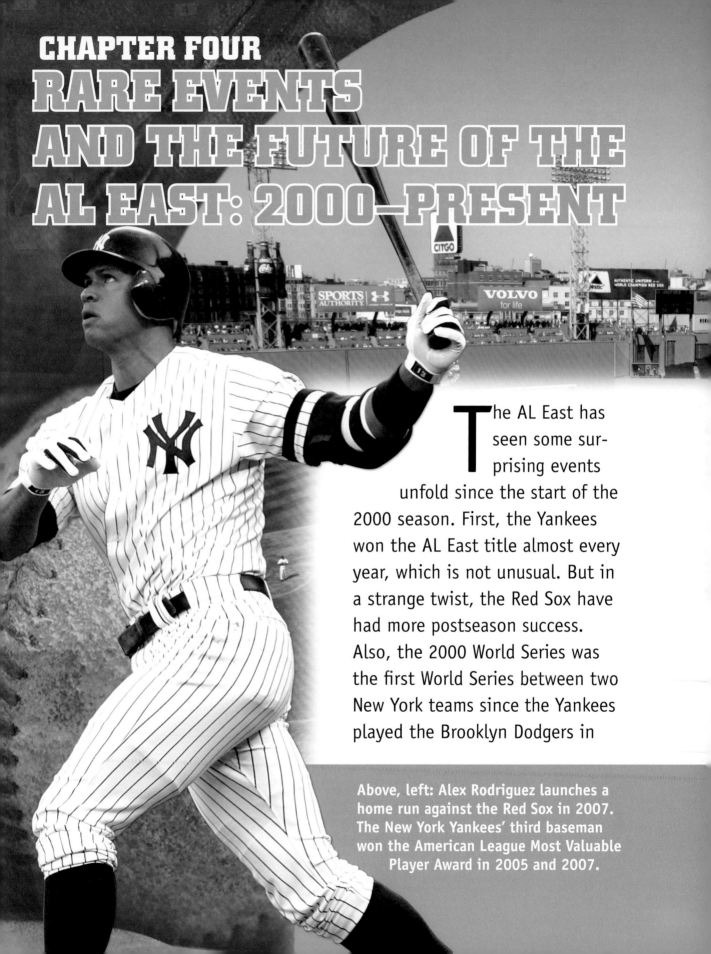

CHAPTER FOUR
RARE EVENTS AND THE FUTURE OF THE AL EAST: 2000–PRESENT

The AL East has seen some surprising events unfold since the start of the 2000 season. First, the Yankees won the AL East title almost every year, which is not unusual. But in a strange twist, the Red Sox have had more postseason success. Also, the 2000 World Series was the first World Series between two New York teams since the Yankees played the Brooklyn Dodgers in

Above, left: Alex Rodriguez launches a home run against the Red Sox in 2007. The New York Yankees' third baseman won the American League Most Valuable Player Award in 2005 and 2007.

1956. And perhaps most surprising of all, in 2004, the Red Sox finally broke the "Curse of the Bambino" by winning the team's first World Series title in 86 years.

The Subway Series

It was an exciting time to be a baseball fan in New York during the 2000 season. For the first time since 1956, the World Series featured two New York City teams, the Yankees and the Mets. The matchup between the Yankees and Mets is called a Subway Series because fans can simply take a short subway ride to get to either stadium. (Back in 1956, many of the players took the subway to the games, too.) The Yankees entered the World Series as favorites and did not disappoint their fans, beating their crosstown rivals four games to one.

Red Sox Break the Curse of the Bambino

Legend has it that the Red Sox have been cursed since the team sold Babe Ruth to the Yankees in 1919. The supposed curse came to be known as the "Curse of the Bambino," after one of Babe Ruth's nicknames. Following Ruth's departure, the Red Sox were unable to win a World Series, losing painful seven-game series in 1946, 1967, 1975, and 1986. While it is impossible to know for sure if the Red Sox really were jinxed, they put an end to such talk in 2004.

In 2004, the Yankees won the AL East and met the wild card–winning Red Sox in the ALCS. The Yankees were ahead in the series, three games to none, and were just one win away from going to the World Series. As improbable as it was, the Red Sox won four straight games to take the series four games to three. They also won the ALCS

Tampa Bay's Carl Crawford slides into home plate before Red Sox catcher Jason Varitek can apply the tag.

Crawford began his career with the Rays in 2002. At the time, he was just 20 years old. Since then, he has gained a reputation as one of the fastest players in the game. Crawford has led the American League in stolen bases four times and was voted to the American League All-Star team in 2004 and 2007.

Alex Ríos: Toronto's All-Star Outfielder

Alex Ríos broke into the league with the Toronto Blue Jays in 2004, at just 23 years old. Defensively, Ríos plays in the outfield. In 2007, he hit an impressive 24 home runs. Ríos was a member of the American League All-Star team in 2006 and 2007. In 2007, Ríos led the Blue Jays in several offensive categories, including batting average, hits, and stolen bases.

Dustin Pedroia: Boston's Star Second Baseman

Just 22 years old at the time, Dustin Pedroia made his debut with the Boston Red Sox in 2006. The second baseman became a star player in 2007. Pedroia batted .317 for the Red Sox and won the AL Rookie of the Year Award. In addition, Pedroia was one of the main contributors to the 2007 World Series winning team.

Nick Markakis: Baltimore's Top Hitter

In 2006, Baltimore Orioles outfielder Nick Markakis emerged as one of baseball's best young hitters. He accomplished a remarkable batting feat that year. On August 22, the 22-year-old rookie hit three home runs in a single game. Markakis continued his impressive hitting in 2007, leading his ball club in hits, home runs, and RBI (runs batted in).

Joba Chamberlain: New York's Prized Pitcher

In 2007, Joba Chamberlain pitched in 19 games for the New York Yankees. Even though Chamberlain appeared in relatively few games, he quickly became a fan favorite. The 21-year-old rookie impressed Yankees fans and frustrated opposing batters with his wicked fastball and nasty slider. Chamberlain struck out 34 batters during the 2007

Best Closer of All Time?

Mariano Rivera is baseball's premier closer. Born in Panama, Rivera debuted with the Yankees in 1995. His pitching statistics place him among the best relief pitchers of all time. Rivera has collected more than 400 saves in his career. In addition, he has been elected to eight All-Star teams. Rivera is probably best known for his incredible post-season accomplishments. He holds many postseason records, including most career postseason saves and most career World Series saves. Rivera is a four-time World Series champion. In 1999, he was named World Series MVP.

Mariano Rivera *(center)* celebrates with his Yankees teammates after they swept the Atlanta Braves in the 1999 World Series.

regular season in only 24 innings pitched. Additionally, he had an impressive 2-0 record with a 0.38 ERA during his first big league season.

The Future of the AL East

It's an exciting time to be a fan of AL East baseball, and there is a lot to look forward to in the future if your favorite team plays in the division. With baseball being a big business, each organization is sure to do whatever it can to put together a fun, interesting, and winning team. The division's established stars will keep on doing their thing, and the young stars and upcoming players will continue to improve to become tomorrow's All-Stars. In short, history will continue to be made.

Carlos Peña is one of the many young stars to watch in the AL East. The hard-hitting Tampa Bay first baseman belted 46 home runs in 2007.

Rays Change Name and Uniform, 2008

Tampa Bay did not record a winning season between 1998 and 2007. However, it appears that a new name and uniform has changed the team's fortunes. Beginning in 2008, the Devil Rays became known simply as the Rays. In addition, the team adopted a new logo and new colors for their uniforms. The Rays' new uniforms are navy blue and white, and their logo is the word "Rays," printed in blue with a small orange sunburst in the opening of the letter R.

New Yankee Stadium Opens, 2009

Yankee Stadium, built in 1923 and known as "the House That Ruth Built," closed down after the 2008 season. The new Yankee Stadium was constructed right across the street from the original. The new stadium includes some of the old stadium's features, such as the iconic white facade. Monument Park, which features plaques of the Yankees' retired numbers and monuments of their greatest players, has also been relocated to the new stadium.

Alex Rodriguez Chases the Career Home Run Record

When Alex Rodriguez hit his 500th home run in 2007, he became the youngest player ever to accomplish the feat. If Rodriguez stays injury-free, many people believe that he has the best chance among active players to break Barry

American League East Division Champs, 1994–2007

1994: Yankees*
1995: Red Sox
1996: Yankees
1997: Orioles
1998: Yankees
1999: Yankees
2000: Yankees
2001: Yankees
2002: Yankees
2003: Yankees
2004: Yankees
2005: Yankees
2006: Yankees
2007: Red Sox

* (Strike-shortened season; no play-offs)

Bonds's career home run record. At the end of the 2007 season, Bonds had hit 762 home runs in his career. In December 2007, Alex Rodriguez signed a ten-year, $275 million contract with the Yankees. The long-term deal almost guarantees that if Rodriguez breaks Bonds's home run record, he would do so in a Yankees uniform.

GLOSSARY

closer Relief pitcher who comes in to get the last out(s) of the game.

debut Player's first appearance in a Major League Baseball game.

dynasty Dominant team in sports over the course of a few years or more.

expansion team A new team that joins a league.

franchise In baseball, an organization or team, along with its name and logo.

Fu Manchu mustache Long mustache with ends that turn down to the chin.

induct To vote into an exclusive club or group.

intimidating Scary, or acting tough in order to gain a competitive edge over an opponent.

no-hitter Game in which a pitcher or combination of pitchers do not allow a single hit in a nine-inning game.

nostalgic Reminding one of feelings of the past.

relief pitcher Pitcher who comes in when the starting pitcher is removed from the game.

rivalry Unusually intense competition between players or teams.

walk-off home run Game-winning home run, always hit by a player for the home team.

Major League Baseball
The Office of the Commissioner of Baseball
245 Park Avenue, 31st Floor
New York, NY 10167
(212) 931-7800
Web site: http://www.mlb.com
The commissioner's office oversees all aspects of Major League
Baseball.

National Baseball Hall of Fame and Museum
25 Main Street
Cooperstown, NY 13326
(888) HALL-OF-FAME (425-5633)
Web site: http://www.baseballhalloffame.org
The National Baseball Hall of Fame and Museum celebrates
and preserves the history of baseball.

Negro Leagues Baseball Museum
1616 East 18th Street
Kansas City, MO 64108
(816) 221-1920
Web site: http://www.nlbm.com
The Negro Leagues Baseball Museum honors great African
American baseball players who were once excluded from
Major League Baseball.

(Note: Links to official team Web sites are available at the Rosenlinks URL, listed below.)

Web Sites

Due to the changing nature of Internet links, Rosen Publishing has developed an online list of Web sites related to the subject of this book. This site is updated regularly. Please use this link to access the list:

http://www.rosenlinks.com/imlb/amle

Christopher, Matt. *World Series: Legendary Sports Events*. New York, NY: Little, Brown & Company, 2007.

Fischer, David. *Baseball Top 10*. New York, NY: DK Publishing, Inc., 2004.

Greenberg, Keith. *Sports Heroes and Legends: Derek Jeter*. New York, NY: Barnes and Noble, 2005.

Lipsyte, Robert. *Heroes of Baseball: The Men Who Made It America's Favorite Game*. New York, NY: Atheneum Books for Young Readers, 2006.

Mulroy, Kevin. *Baseball as America: Seeing Ourselves Through Our National Game*. Washington, DC: National Geographic Society, 2005.

Sandler, Michael. *Baseball: The 2004 Boston Red Sox*. New York, NY: Bearport Publishing Company, Inc., 2005.

Stewart, Mark. *New York Yankees*. Chicago, IL: Norwood House Press, 2007.

Wong, Stephen. *Baseball Treasures*. New York, NY: HarperCollins, 2007.

BIBLIOGRAPHY

Baseball Almanac. "Division Series History." Retrieved April 7, 2008 (http://www.baseball-almanac.com/division_series/division_series.shtml).

Baseball Reference. "Most Valuable Player Awards and Cy Young Award Winners." Retrieved April 9, 2008 (http://www.baseball-reference.com/awards/mvp_cya.shtml).

Frommer, Harvey. *Yankee Century and Beyond*. Naperville, IL: Sourcebooks, Inc., 2006.

James, Bill. *The New Bill James Historical Baseball Abstract*. New York, NY: Simon and Schuster, 2003.

Kahn, Roger. *October Men: Reggie Jackson, George Steinbrenner, Billy Martin, and the Yankees' Miraculous Finish in 1978*. New York, NY: Harcourt, 2004.

Lieb, Frederick G. *Baltimore Orioles: The History of a Colorful Team in Baltimore and St. Louis*. Carbondale, IL: Southern Illinois University Press, 2005.

Lowry, Phillip J. *Green Cathedrals: The Ultimate Celebration of All Major League and Negro League Ballparks*. New York, NY: Walker and Company, 2006.

Lyle, Sparky, with Peter Golenbock. *Bronx Zoo: The Astonishing Inside Story of the 1978 World Champion New York Yankees*. Chicago, IL: Triumph Books, 2005.

National Baseball Hall of Fame and Museum. "The Hall of Famers." Retrieved April 9, 2008 (http://www.web.baseballhalloffame.org/hofers).

Shaughnessy, Dan. *Curse of the Bambino*. New York, NY: Penguin Group, 2004.

Stewart, Mark, and James L. Gates. *The Boston Red Sox*. Chicago, IL: Norwood House Press, 2006.

Tan, Cecilia. *The 50 Greatest Yankee Games*. Hoboken, NJ: John Wiley and Sons, Inc., 2006.

Vecsey, George. *Baseball: A History of America's Favorite Game*. New York, NY: Random House Publishing Group, 2006.

INDEX

About the Author

Matt Monteverde is a writer currently living in Summit, New Jersey. He graduated from Rutgers University in 2003 with a bachelor's degree in sociology. Monteverde has written several young adult books on a wide variety of topics, including teenage violence, budgeting and money management, and the Iraq War. He is an avid baseball enthusiast.

Photo Credits

Cover (all photos), pp. 1 (all photos), 4–5, 7 (both photos), 16 (both photos), 23 (both photos), 26, 27, 31 (both photos), 33 © Getty Images; p. 3, back cover © www.istockphotos.com/Nhuan Nguyen; pp. 7 (foreground), 17 © Focus on Sports/Getty Images; pp. 10, 13 © MLB Photos via Getty Images; pp. 14, 18, 30, 35, 37, 38 © AP Photos; p. 21 © AFP/Getty Images.

Designer: Sam Zavieh; Editor: Christopher Roberts
Photo Researcher: Marty Levick